Songs From Over the Event Horizon

Anne Geraghty

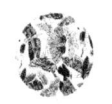

For Life

CONTENTS

1. The Songs — 6
2. The Anthropocene — 10
3. Extinction is Forever — 14
4. Why Do We Look the Other Way? — 18
5. What Have We Done? — 22
6. The Matrix of Power — 26
7. Gazing Into the Void — 30
8. The Rest Is Silence — 34
9. False Hope Is Now a Form of Denial — 38
10. Through the Labyrinth — 42
11. The Wisdom of the Body — 46
12. The Politics of Experience — 50
13. Lost and Found — 54
14. Instinctual Love — 58
15. The Sacred Body — 62
16. From Here to Eternity — 66
17. Love's Body — 70
18. Beyond Tragedy — 74
19. The Song — 78
20. Beetles — 80

Songs From Over the Event Horizon is a song-poem written for **Still Moving**, a dance theatre company, to perform with music and images. It is a living celebration of life on Earth and a lament for the natural world that is being destroyed.

We have been activists working to support life on Earth for over 50 years. Our initial youthful enthusiasm gave way to the more grounded realisation that preventing catastrophe was going to be far harder than we imagined. However we continued to hope enough people would wake up to the depth of the eco-crisis so that humanity could come together and deal intelligently with this serious threat to life. Over years it became apparent this was not going to happen. We had to gaze into the void and acknowledge that we were facing a mass extinction event that was not going to be averted. What do you do when you have no more hope?

For a long time we were angry, heartbroken and in despair. We went looking in all directions for guidance and inspiration. We learned from the wisdom of plants, the teachings of animals and the instinctual knowledge within our own bodies. We eventually reached new understandings about life, death and extinction, and found a different kind of hope. This is a song-poem about what we discovered. We hope it helps you as it has us.

Anne Geraghty

This is not an easy read. It can overwhelm you if you read it on your own. So here are a few suggestions to help with the reading of it.

It is a song-poem so read it aloud or as if aloud so you can feel its rhythm and pulse. And read it in sections rather than all at once.

It helps to read it standing, this way your body can move while reading. Imagine you are in front of an audience and are giving the poem to them.

Read it with others, each taking a paragraph at a time. This creates a dynamic between you in the reading. Read the choruses and the final song together.

Imagine dancers and actors moving and expressing some of the actions/scenarios, with images of what is being described portrayed on screens behind you.

If you want to put on a performance event for others using this song-poem, then feel free. (Unless you are a wealthy Hollywood or West End producer in which case you can pay for the rights.) Music and images will be available for those who want to use these in an event of some kind. Contact us for this: info@stillmovingcompany.co.uk

Last but not at all least - have fun with it. Create your own way of reading. When you reach the end you'll understand why we felt we had to do this.

Martin Gerrish, Still Moving Company

Songs From Over the Event Horizon

The Songs

Can you hear the songs?
Can you hear them in the calling of geese and the barks of dogs,
In the songs of larks and the croaks of frogs,
In the roars of tigers and the grunts of bears,
In the howls of wolves and the pants of hares,
In the rustle of beetles and the meows of cats
In the whispers of spiders and the chirps of bats,
In the flight of owls and the breathing of whales,
In the slithers of snakes and the crawling of snails,
In the clicks of dolphins and the snuffling of moles,
In the quarrels of sparrows and the squeaking of voles?

Let's walk over the hills and swim in the songs of lakes.
Let's sing with the rivers, the stones, the fish and the snakes.
Let's lie in singing grass and sing with beetles and bugs,
And sing the songs of mushrooms, insects, hedgehogs and slugs.
Let's leave the city and take the road into the woods,
And sing with the trees songs of fires and floods.
Let's make a home where the sky meets the land,
And dance under the moon on singing sands.

Let's make music with octopuses, skylarks, lynx and baboons,
Sing songs with platypuses, aardvarks, minks and raccoons.
Let's kneel in fields, smell the soil and sing songs with the ground.
Let's sing the songs we lost and then found again in the sound.
Let's sing these songs of anarchy, laughter and terrible cruelty,
Savage magnificence, fierce love and dark unbearable beauty.
For how do we live our wild and precious lives on Earth
If we do not sing of the tragedy of death as well as the joys of birth?

Now let's sing and be sung by these songs of wonder and dread.
But sing them while you're alive - because you can't when you're dead.
Sing until your heart breaks and you are left bereft.
Sing until you can sing no more and have no song left.
Sing until you're so lost in the song
You've sung yourself back to where you belong.
Sing until you no longer sing the song,
The song sings you - as it has done all along.
Then leap up and dance in the wind and the rain,
And sing the songs of the wild - and then sing them again.

The Anthropocene

But there's something happening we need to explore,
Something vital, urgent, important and raw.
A dark wind is blowing a great evil,
That brings destruction, catastrophe and is deadly lethal.

Humanity has known great suffering in famines and in war
But we've never encountered a tragedy on this scale before.
It's the worst reality ever to confront humanity,
The extinction of life - the ultimate tragedy.

Scientists say this vast dying, in which nearly all life will end,
Is a bio-catastrophe almost impossible to comprehend.
And the devastation of this sixth mass extinction
Will be a fate worse than any dystopian fiction.

Indigenous cultures have witnessed and known for a long time,
The industrial world commits environmental crimes.
They can see this apocalyptic disaster is a dystopian darkness,
That will ruin, destroy and indelibly harm us.
Yet they are powerless and this catastrophe is not of their making,
So they suffer and watch while their hearts are breaking.

If you believe we should always be positive,
You'll find what follows raw and provocative.
Yet to deal with this crisis we must be grounded in reality,
Not lost in delusional hope or escapist fantasies.

But if we conquer fear and gaze into the heart of this darkness,
We'll release the love and awareness in a healing catharsis
That we need to navigate the approaching catastrophes
With grounded intelligence and creative strategies.

So now let's explore the unfolding global tragedy,
Without denying the gravity of this tragic calamity.

ESEMPHE TUMI

Esemphe Tumi

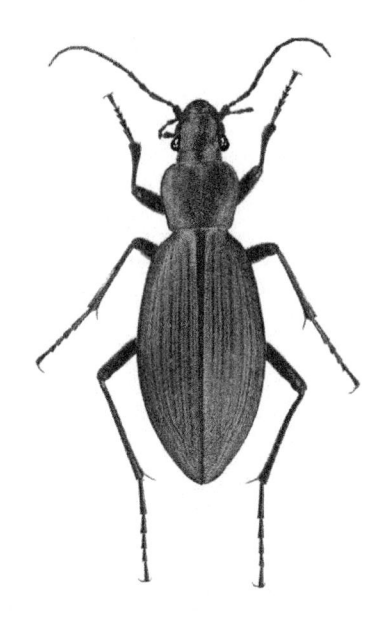

Chilean Magnificent Beetle

Ceroglossus Chilensis

Extinction is Forever

Professor Ceballos and an international team
Wrote the following in 2017:
'We are well into a sixth mass extinction.
It is difficult to appreciate that this decimation
Will be the biological annihilation, that cannot be reversed,
Of the only assemblage of life we know of in the universe.'

Though written by eminent scientists,
It was met with an ominous silence.

This mass extinction is called the Anthropocene,
A word that means 'caused by human beings.'
Because what's led to this apocalyptic calamity
Is our human ignorance and collective insanity.

Action to stop this catastrophe is vital
Yet we continue as if indisputably entitled
To use and abuse the Earth's resources,
Kill the animals and pollute the waters,
Burn the rainforest and chop down trees,
Deep trawl the ocean and empty out the seas,
Destroy habitats, trash ecosystems,
Drop dirty bombs on innocent victims,
Melt the ice caps, turn fields to desert,
Deny the statistics, ignore the experts,
Factory farm animals, devastate the countryside,
Contaminate with pesticides, spray with insecticide,
Mine mountains, drill for oil,
Ruin lakes, spoil the soil,
Poison the rivers, obliterate wilderness,
And wreck this beautiful Earth with our arrogant wilfulness.

Chorus:
This eco-crisis is about more than global warming and changes in the weather,
It's about the end of life and a dire warning: extinction is forever.

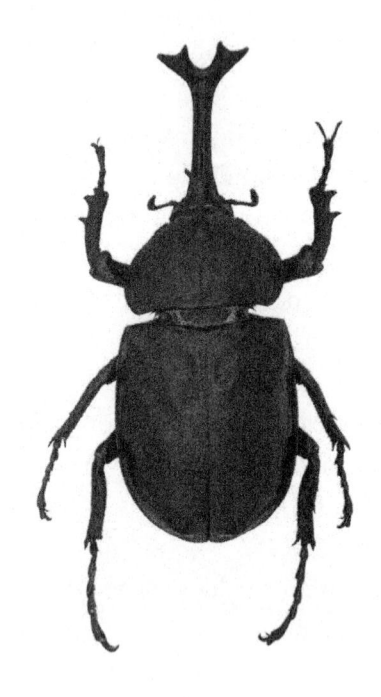

JAPANESE RHINOCEROS BEETLE

Trypoxylus Dichotomus

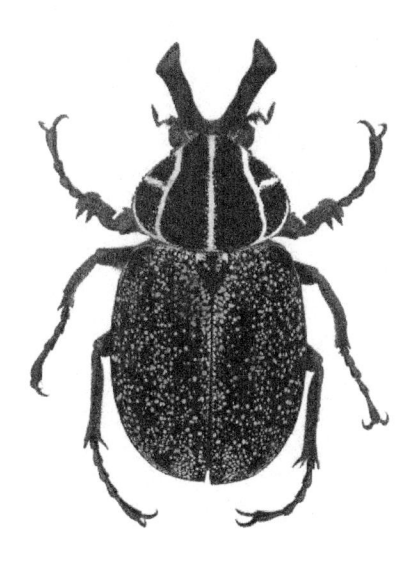

STARRY FLOWER BEETLE

Inca Clathrata Sommeri

Why Do We Look the Other Way?

None of us knows the answers but one thing is sure,
We need radical changes to society, and a whole lot more.
As the eco-crisis takes hold and things fall apart,
We need to gaze into the darkness of our own human hearts.

Why do we ignore the evidence and continue to deny
The approaching eco-apocalypse in which most of us will die?

Perhaps we think it's the job of the politicians
To make the necessary changes and create the transition.

Perhaps we suffer under the irresponsible delusion
That someone else will somehow discover the solution.

Perhaps we don't want to face the reality we're all going to die
So we pray to be saved by a false god in the sky.

Perhaps we've put our faith in a different delusion,
A techno-utopian fantasy of a scientific solution.

Perhaps we believe it's our inalienable individual freedom
To buy whatever we want and have lots of children.

Perhaps we believe we can meditate through this
Into a higher vibration of serenity and bliss.

Perhaps we don't want to give up our desires and addictions
And that's why we ignore these dire predictions.

Perhaps we're simply too afraid to face,
The natural world around us is in dire straits.

But whatever the reason there's a blanket refusal
To do little other than carry on as usual.

Chorus:
Why are so many in denial that soon we'll all be gone
Into the vastness of a void that goes on and on and on?

JEWEL BEETLE

Polybothris Auriventris

ELEPHANTESQUE DUNG BEETLE

Elephastomus Proboscideus

What Have We Done?

We can recycle clothes, stop burning coal and insulate our homes,
We can eat vegan, drive an electric car and glue ourselves to roads,
We can lobby MPs, infiltrate Davos and organise demonstrations,
Yet whatever we do, whatever we try, nothing really changes.

Despite all our campaigns, petitions and endless debates,
Current extinctions are 10,000 greater than the background rate.
There's no point denying that life is in dire straits,
And the natural world is dying at alarming rates.

In 1992 the 1st Earth Summit was full of hope and optimism.
At the 2nd, 10 years later, there was fear and pessimism -
Nearly every environmental problem identified had got worse.
Another 10 years on, even the few gains had gone into reverse.

There was no sign of this cataclysmic destruction changing.
The conclusion was, we had virtually no time remaining.

At Aichi, twenty-four international biodiversity targets were set.
Ten years later not a single goal in any nation had been met.
Another 10 years later every nation had again failed every goal.
The corporate-industrial-military complex will not be controlled.

At Cop26 an agreement to halt deforestation
Was signed by Brazil and every other nation.
Since there's a 70% increase in rainforest destruction in Brazil
And not a single promise by any nation has been fulfilled.

Explore what's really going on and you will be shocked
That the political and industrial world will not be stopped.
You hear about the agreements but little about the failures.
Meanwhile nature is being annihilated by our ruinous behaviour.

We've created a global killing machine and must take responsibility
For the mega technologies poisoning life with their hyper-toxicity.
This is why we need to talk about the deeper meta-politics,
And the four evil horsemen of this eco-apocalypse.

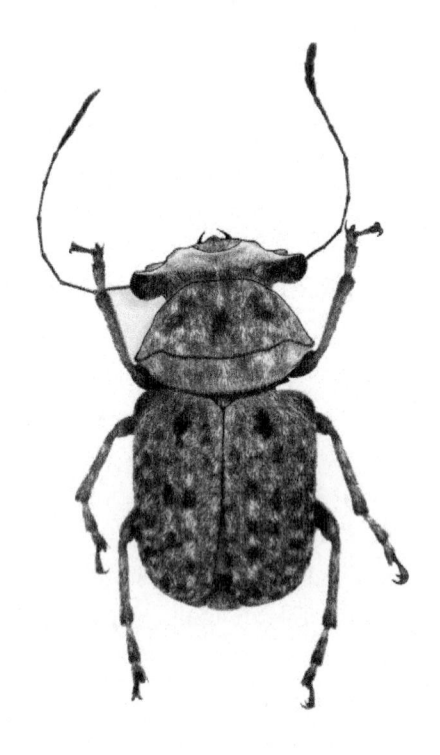

Cow-Faced Anthribid

Exechesops Leucopis

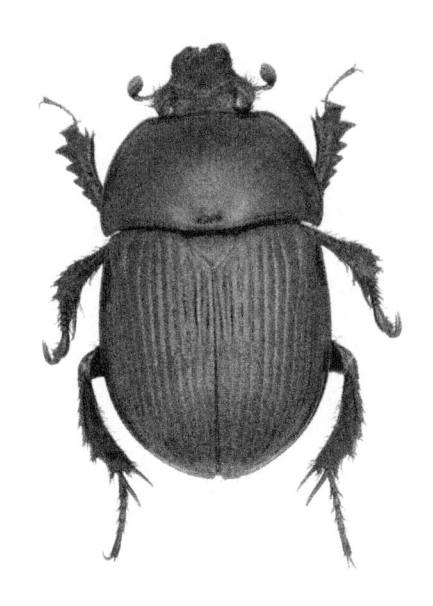

Splendid Earth-Boring Beetle

Geotrupes Splendidus

The Matrix of Power

The **1st**: The vast international industrial-military complex
And the collective insanity that gives war meaning and context.
We've enough nuclear warheads, bio-weapons and atomic bombs,
Intercontinental missiles, submarines and thermobaric bombs,
To totally destroy the global ecosystem in the MAD dysfunction
That continues to stockpile these weapons of mass destruction.

The **2nd**: The global super-predator that hunts, farms and kills
Billions of animals annually just for money or the thrill.
A relentless massacre for which there's no excuse
That kills apex predators at 9 times the rate they reproduce.
Even if this ceased tomorrow, they can't recover from this abuse,
Their gene pool has been irreversibly and catastrophically reduced.

The **3rd**: The profit motive, mass consumerism and corporate greed
That sells material forms of happiness in things we do not need.
So we chain ourselves to desks selling things we later buy
With the money we made selling them and never ask 'Why?'
We're trapped in a global machine, believing what we've been told.
Thinking we are free when that's another dream we've been sold.

The 4th: Our belief in the superiority of the intellectual mind
Means respect for our fellow creatures is seriously undermined.
We destroy without reflection the natural world that maintains us.
Though it's hardly intelligent to destroy what sustains us.
Our arrogant speciesism thinks because we give the animals names
This means we are above them, but at root we are the same.
We believe we belong to ourselves but that is just our ignorance
We also belong to each other - a deeper and different intelligence.

There's a fifth and equally dangerous horseman of destruction
The source of much deceit and awful corruption.
But we'll go into that disturbing truth later
When exploring further the depths of human nature.

Chorus:
We can no longer avoid gazing into the void,
And seeing how much of life we have already destroyed.

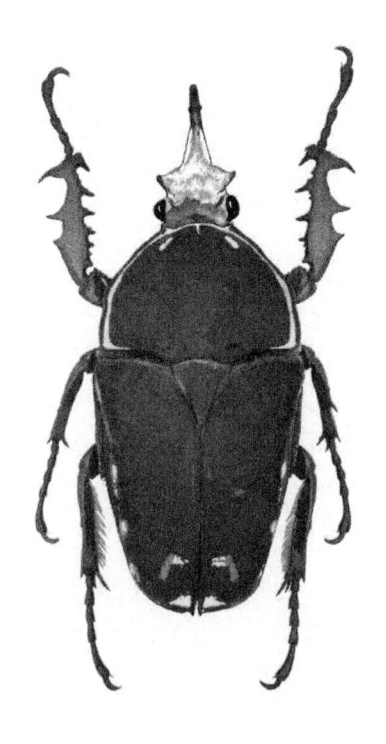

UGANDAN FLOWER BEETLE

Mecynorhina Torqhata

CONVERGENT LADY BEETLE

Hippodamia Covergens

Gazing Into the Void

David Attenborough described humans as a plague upon the Earth,
Who've spread disease and death like a mediaeval curse.
We represent less than 0.01% of the 9 million species living
Yet have killed 85% of life through hunting, farming and fishing.
38% of all mammals are now human, 60% are farmed,
Only 2% are wild - and each day more are harmed.

Every day the oil industry makes 2.8 billion dollars profit
Whatever scientists or politicians say, they're not going to stop it.
They knew the danger 70y ago but didn't care or see the necessity.
They're happy with the 52 trillion they've made since 1970.

But it's not only the industries of fossil fuels and oil,
75% of Earth's land is now degraded soil.
Soil can be worth more than what grows in it yet we treat it like dirt.
We lose 100 million hectares of land per year - this is going to hurt.
In less than 30 years 90% of land will be close to desertification
Leading to a serious food crisis in every single nation.

200 species of animals, plants and flowers
Are driven to extinction by human activity every 24 hours.
In less than 30 years, we're on track to lose
90% of all wild life – but that's not reported in the news.

Nearer home you may have noticed insects are hardly seen.
Thousands used to fly onto our car windscreens.
In the morning sun, spider's webs hung glistening in the trees
Among masses of butterflies, dragon flies, ladybirds and bees.
In less than 20 years we've lost 65% in an insect Apocalypse,
The far-reaching catastrophe of an appalling collapse.

Insects feed the world; when they go, the world starves.
Few listened over 60y ago when 'Silent Spring' sounded the alarm.
Already the dawn chorus is quieter, the loss of song severe.
In the UK we've lost 114 million birds in the last 50 years.
30 million house sparrows, 4 million skylarks, 20 million starlings,
Gone because of habitat loss, pollution, and industrial farming.

It's clear to those of us who care, the behemoths of power
Will preserve their vested interests and the Earth will be devoured.

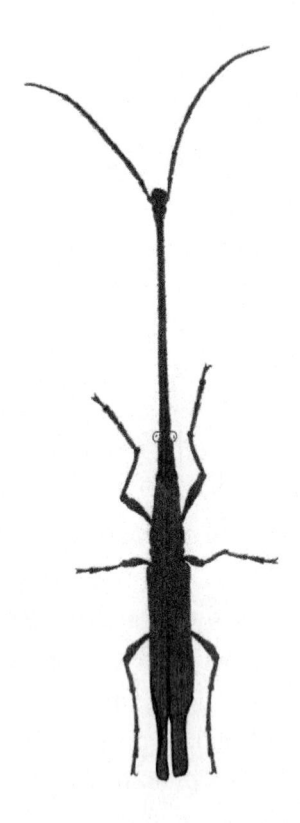

Giraffe Weevil

Lasiorhynchus Barbicornis

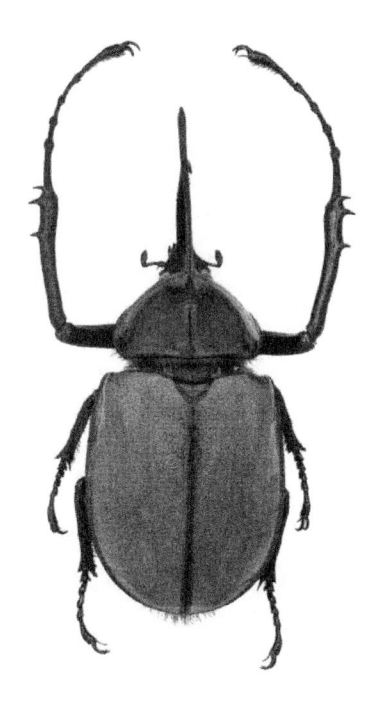

Rhinoceros Beetle

Golofa Porteri

The Rest Is Silence

The warning signs are clear, the message, stark,
There's no point pretending the future isn't dark.
Ahead lie anarchy, terror, fires, floods, and violence,
Starvation, mass migration, mega-deaths, and a vast empty silence.

We're set for the dark side of the moon & into the heart of the sun.
Even the rich and powerful will not escape this one,
Because we're taking down with us into the night of oblivion
Birds, insects, mammals, fish, reptiles and amphibians.

All will be lost and never found,
Gone into a dark flight down,
Into the abysmal void of that infernal region,
The tenth circle of hell - eternal oblivion.

Where there'll be no more baboons, beavers, bats or cats,
No raccoons, retrievers, rats or gnats,
No auks, dolphins, moles or snails,
No hawks, terrapins, voles or whales,
No rays, gorillas, bugs or bees,
No jays, chinchillas, slugs or fleas,
No kangaroos, caribous, gnus or moths,
No cockatoos, kinkajous, shrews or sloths,
No eels, bears, hippopotamuses or dogs,
No seals, hares, rhinoceroses or frogs,
No octopuses, ferrets, lynx or clams,
No platypuses, parrots, minks or lambs,
No dingoes, skylarks, monkeys or mice,
No flamingos, aardvarks, donkeys or lice,
No foxes, drakes, camels or worms,
No oxen, snakes, mammals or germs,
No chicks, no hens and no orangutans,
No ticks, no wrens, and no woman and no man.

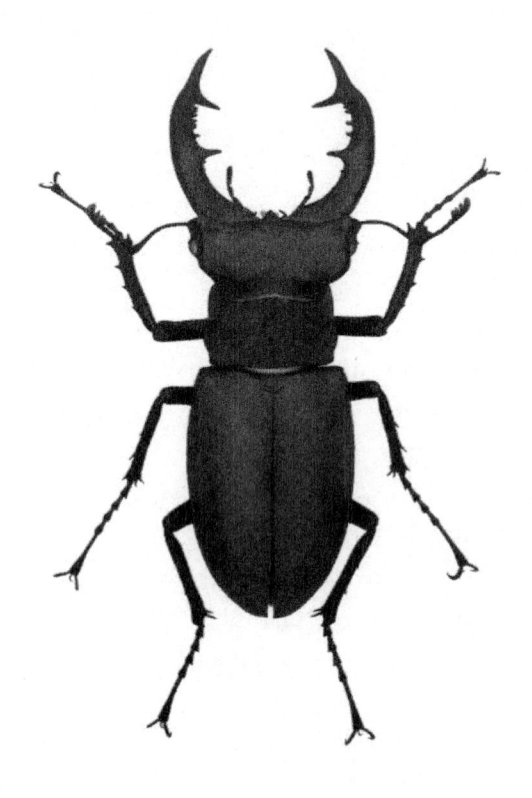

GOLDEN STAG BEETLE

Odontolabis Cuvera

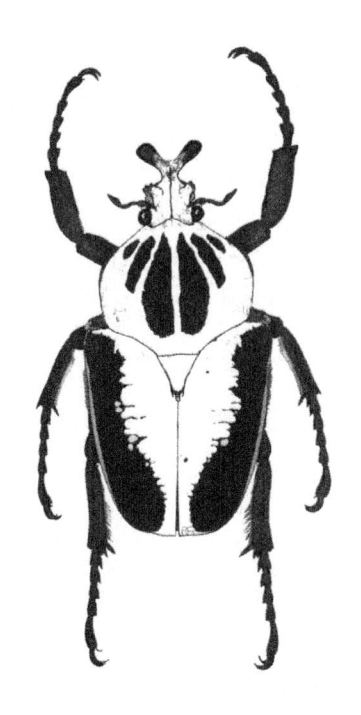

ROYAL GOLIATH BEETLE

Goliathus Regius

39

False Hope is Now a Form of Denial

You might say we need hope else we'll fall into despair,
But it doesn't help to be deluded, in denial and unaware.
And when it comes to hunger and raw survival
False hope is now a form of denial.

Our challenge is no longer how to prevent this devastation
And its mega-threat to life and human civilisation,
It has become how to navigate this with compassion and integrity,
Creating a different kind of hope with love and sincerity.

We need a geo-political psycho-spiritual revolution
To have any hope at all of finding a solution.
And we need to take action now not simply hope and wait
Until the catastrophes are upon us and it's all too late.
So what can we do and how might we embark
On dealing with all this and building our arks?

We might grow food on common land in teams
Sharing our different skills and expertise.
We might follow an urge to leave the city behind
And take off on an adventure, not knowing what we'll find.

We might create our own community, far from the madding crowd,
Where we explore with impunity and new freedoms are allowed.
We might spend time enjoying the endless wonders of nature
And marvel at the resourcefulness of our fellow earth creatures.
We might meditate and tune into subtle body energies,
And live in the present not in future dreams or past memories.
We might create a collective to buy a farm
Where we are self sufficient and live away from harm.
We might move through the frontiers of our analytical intellect
And realise many of our ideas are hypocritical and incorrect.
We might celebrate life in theatre and dance, sing songs, create art,
Make films, write poetry and music, to express what's in our hearts.
We might tune into and learn from our instinctive intelligence
And discover, in this eco-crisis, our instincts are more relevant.
We might be careful about having children and creating a family
In a world that will descend increasingly into anarchy and insanity.
We might sit and weep over our dreadful mistakes
And let life itself guide us while our collective hearts break.
We might wild swim in rivers, strip naked and dance.
We might tune into the wisdom of mushrooms and plants.
We might decide with courage and fearlessness
To leave the world behind and live deep in wilderness.
For each of us our journey will be different;
Some parts will be hell, some, magnificent.
Though to carry us through the fast approaching dark,
Our love of life will help us build our arks.

Chorus:
But whatever our path through the cataclysmic times ahead
We need to deal with it now because we can't when we're dead.

Cossyphus Hoffmannseggii

Cossyphus Hoffmannseggi

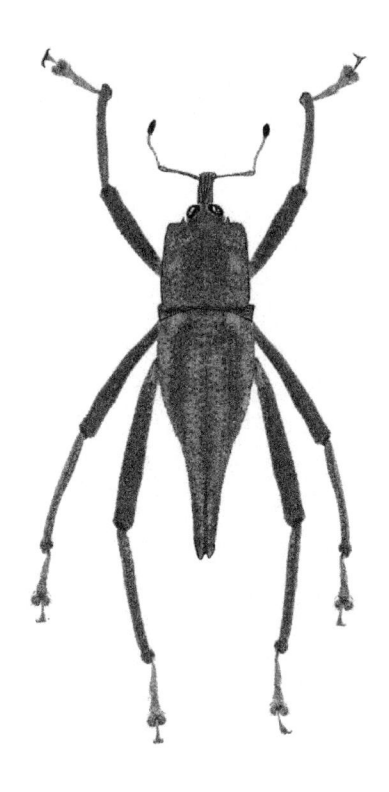

Spider Weevil

Arachnobas Caudatus

43

Through the Labyrinth

We might be a graffiti artist or a Reiki healer,
A concert pianist or a drug dealer,
A schoolteacher or a subsistence farmer,
A zookeeper or a Tibetan Lama,
A taxi driver, a city mayor,
A fashion buyer or a poker player,
A deep-sea diver, a coal miner,
A famous writer, or a mountain climber,
A bicycle courier, political activist,
Criminal lawyer or digital analyst,
A radical separatist feminist
Or a single mother on benefits,
But we each have to find our unique way through the labyrinth,
Some of us team players, some of us mavericks.
But whatever way forward or action we decide,
Life itself must be our mentor and guide.
Consoling fantasies and relentless positivity
Help no one in the end - we need the substance of reality.

Yet so many anti-life dynamics are entrenched in the human mind,
It seems only a shock can unearth the alleged wisdom of our kind.
We need the depth of the tragedy to shock us awake,
So we stop hiding from our collective mistakes.

The most fantastic construction of the human mind
Has been the creation of the world - but we are blind.
We can't see the survival of the world is costing us our lives.
But do we want the world or do we want life? We need to decide.

To choose life we must detoxify from our hyper materialism,
Our deadly desires, addictions and species imperialism,
Face our fear, be spontaneous, dare to love and take the risk
To disentangle from the conditioning of the global cultural matrix,
Go beyond the ego and its addiction to power and control,
And open to what is greater than us, and surrender to the whole.

Forked Fungus Beetle

Bolitotherus Cornutus

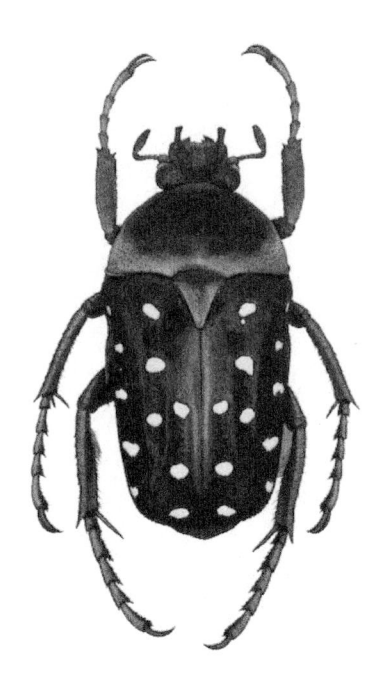

MISTLETOE BEETLE

Stephanorrhina Guttata

The Wisdom of the Body

We think of the body as an object, but the body is not a thing;
It is life, energy, movement and continuously changing.
Out of this flow of energy we create a world of discreet objects,
Each existing separately within its own unique context.

But this objectified universe is only one reality,
Another is that we are all one river, including humanity.
The intellectual mind forgets this but the body knows,
Life is far more mysterious than we think or suppose.

The ego of the world needs to surrender to a different wisdom,
That of the body and the instincts of the animal kingdom.
We need to listen to our bodies for what we truly need
Not just for what we think we want out of ego, fear and greed.
We need to detach from the capitalist materialist conditioning
That bombards us with images of the good life via consumerism.

We need to find the natural happiness we knew as children,
And this joy still lives in us and is not really hidden.
It's just we've been conditioned to think accumulating wealth
Is more important than freedom, laughter, love and health.
But the vested interests of the capitalist machine, let's be honest,
Doesn't want us to be happy - they'd then lose all their profits.

We need to wake up to the collective ignorance and folly
That has rejected and ignored the wisdom of the body.
Any animal that neglects the body and its natural instincts
Undermines its life force and soon becomes extinct.
Just as any species that betrays its young
Betrays itself, and that's what we've done.
Which is why, in this Anthropocene age,
We're facing the end of our world – unless we radically change.

Chorus:
And it's not just humanity we're taking down into the dark night of oblivion,
It's the beauty of insects, mammals, birds, fish, reptiles and amphibians.
This crisis is of the body of life itself, literally what matters;
The body of our own life therefore holds many of the answers.

Devil's Coach Horse

Creophilus Erythrocephalus

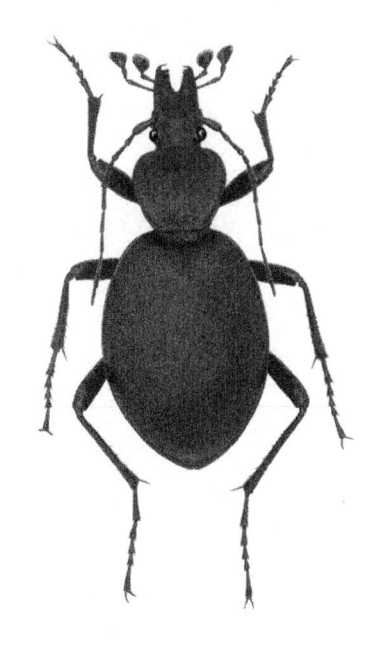

SNAIL HUNTER BEETLE

Cychrus Caraboides

The Politics of Experience

It's not only life out there we need to face and feel,
It's our own life force we need to keep real.
As children we had to fragment our natural animal integrity
In order to enter the society and culture of rational humanity.
We'd be punished and expelled from every nursery and school
If we continued to bite friends, steal toys and grab another's food.
So we divided ourselves from the flow of our natural existence
And abandoned our spontaneity and our animal instincts.

But rules and ideas of duty and morality
Can never incorporate the spontaneous anarchy
Of the animal body and its instinctual energy
With its evolutionary wisdom and genetic memory.
So to develop true wholeness, mature integrity and authenticity,
We must return to our animal roots - our spontaneous simplicity.

Which means we feel it all, our anger, sadness, joy and tears,
Our sexuality, our shame, our laughter and our fears,
Our phobias, our fear of death and existential anxiety,
All the feelings we had to bury to join civilised society.

We play out within us the same dynamics we enact on nature,
And oppress our spontaneous energy like a mini dictator.
Through the fear and ignorance of a collective insanity
We imprison the animal-ness of our natural humanity.
We incarcerate our instinctive energy in a fearful detention
And keep our natural selves trapped in a cage of muscular tension.
The collective ego of the world, in its ignorance, fear and greed,
Imprisons our animal-body - the beast must now be freed.

We need a new paradigm of being to reclaim our bio-inheritance,
Liberate our energy with its instinctive intelligence,
Release the animal body from our ego control,
And free our natural life force to create and grow our soul.

And we need our collective soul more than ever before
To live with integrity through the crisis we can no longer ignore.

Chorus:
Our soul is not something that pre-exists our birth;
It's forged in the blood and loves of a life on planet Earth.

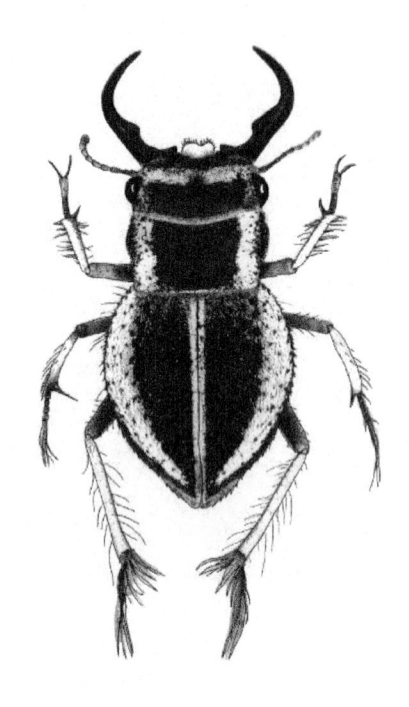

Stag Darkling Beetle

Calognathus Chevrolati Eberlanzi

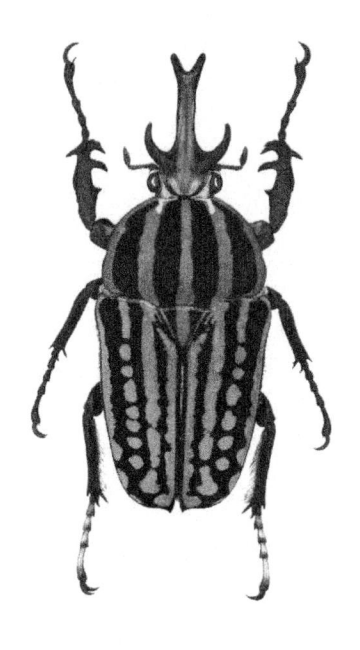

Savage Flower Beetle

Mecynorhina Savegei

Lost and Found

A fish swims blissfully unaware and with no notion
That all around her is water in the vastness of an ocean.
A wave washes her onto the beach.
The life saving water is out of reach.
She is gasping for breath and dying on the sand,
Until another wave washes her home - this time she understands.
She's welcomed back by the sea as a long lost daughter
Because now she is aware of and loves the water.

We are that fish and have a certain knowledge
Though not the facts and theories you learn in college.
We learned how to control ourselves and developed language,
Which gave us technologies, power over life and a great advantage.
We built pyramids, spaceships, roads and cities
But paid a great price in the loss of our abilities
To remain attuned to the instinctive connection with life
That informed our ancestors and helped them survive.

The other animals never left the instinctual bliss of Eden,
But we began a long journey into a different kind of freedom.
One that led to an extremely important and precious creation,
Forged in the heart of our amazing civilisation.
Rather than just breathing, moving and eating in order to survive,
We've created an awareness of life and a consciousness we are alive.

We need to connect this hard won knowledge
With ancient instinctive wisdoms
And share it with our fellow creatures
In the plant and animal kingdoms.
We need to bring to them these gifts of the human spirit
So that even if we don't survive, life itself can benefit.

The imprints and remnants of our civilisation
Can then be for the future a source of nurture and inspiration.
We can leave legacies of freedom, love, beauty, truth and laughter
To the energy fields of existence and whatever life comes after.
Even if some of that legacy will be a dire warning
About the dangers of pollution, exploitation and global warming.
Then, despite the harm of our techno-politico-economic system,
That same system can give to life our consciousness and wisdom.

Chorus:
Our collective betrayal of the animal body is our greatest gift and greatest curse.
Nothing could be more magnificent, and nothing could be worse.

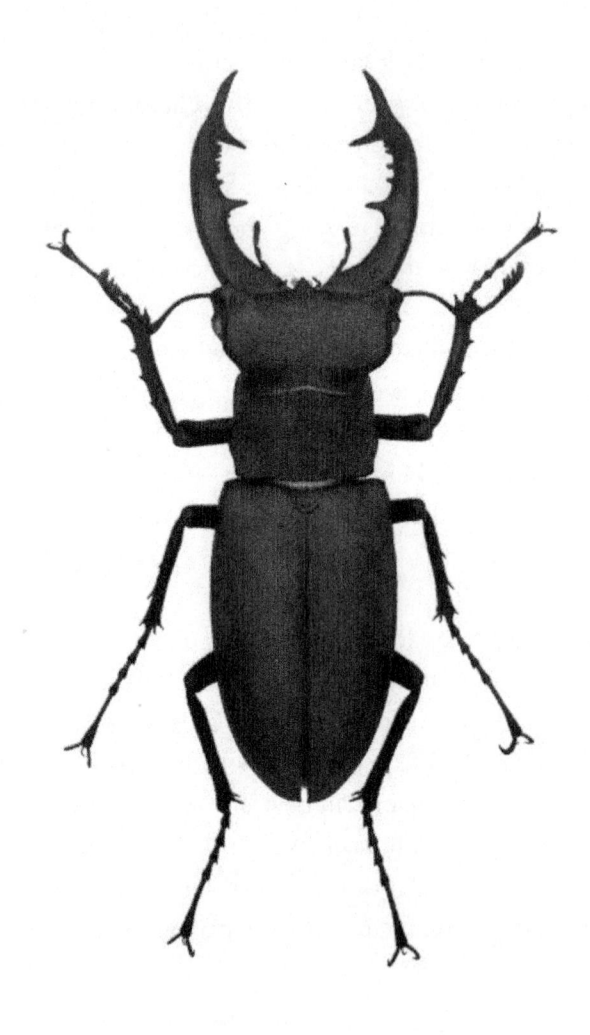

Giant Stag Beetle

Lucanus Elaphus

Cherry Weevil

Rhynchites Auratus

Instinctual Love

One thing we'll discover as the catastrophes rise
Is how deeply we loved life but didn't realise
Until too late - and then our hearts will be broken.
But a broken heart is a heart that is open.
You don't know what you've got 'til it's gone and our alienation
Has created a deeper love of life through our very separation.

We love life all the more because we know what it is to lose it,
Though it's a hard road and few would voluntarily choose it.
Yet through our alienation from our animal nature
We create a love and awareness that is all the greater.
And our journey of loss and rediscovery has a potent consequence.
Through us, the universe creates self-awareness and consciousness.

This makes existence more than a state of being,
It's a creative force that produces love and gives life meaning.

Love is not something that mysteriously pre-existed existence
With its source in some divine being, omnipotent and omniscient.
Love was born in the hearts of mammals and their warm blood,
When their vulnerable young needed attachment, care and love.
This warm bonding ensured their offspring survived.
Altruism and empathy then evolved - and finally love arrived.

We ourselves came alive through the lovemaking of our parents,
Their animal bodies gave us life and our biological inheritance.
The body of love that nurtures and sustains us all
Has its source in the living bodies of creatures great and small.

Chorus:
What creates and sustains us is not a God beyond the stars,
It's the love of us living animals and our warm mammalian hearts.

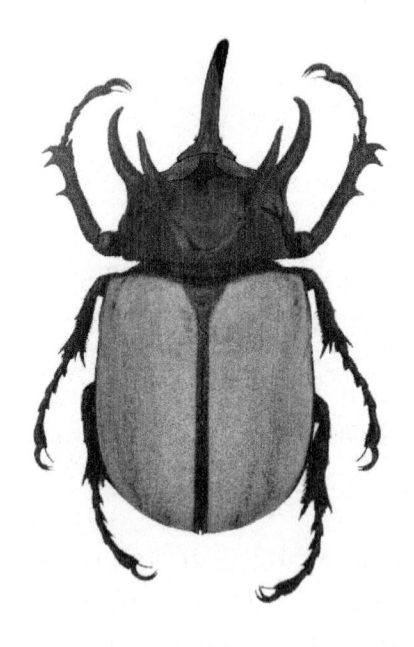

Five-Horned Rhinoceros Beetle

Eupatorus Gracilicornis

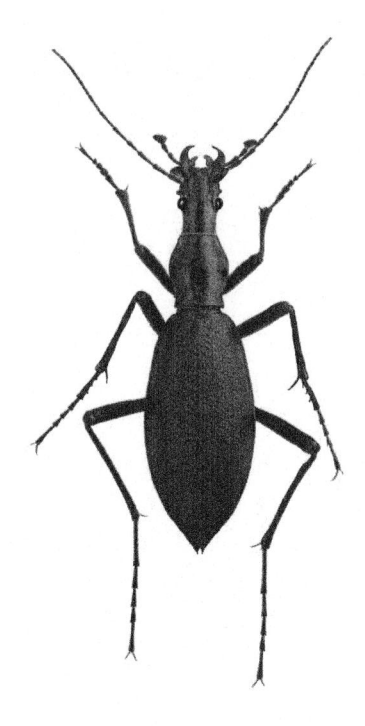

SNAIL-EATING GROUND BEETLE

Damaster Blaptoides

The Sacred Body

The greatest story ever told, that of life on Earth,
Is written into us in the nine months before our birth.
A human embryo grows gills, wings, webbed feet, tails and horns,
All stages of evolution emerge then fade before we are born.

Our DNA holds the truth, we are of the family of mammalians,
And our fellow creatures are our kith and kin, not dangerous aliens.
Our mega-technologies have obliterated this connection,
As a consequence we've lost our ultimate protection.
Because instincts evolved not just for the survival of the individual,
But to keep everything in balance and protect the wider ecosystem.

Each animal and plant is separate, individual, unique and distinct.
Yet we eat and become each other and are completely interlinked.
The flow of this vast river of life and death is the only sacred entity,
In which our belonging to each other holds our deeper identity.

But the spirit that belongs to the life of the animal, religions stole,
And gave it to an abstract disembodied concept of a soul,
That lives forever in an imaginary after-life that is somehow
Worth more than the animal body that is living here and now.
Yet a snorting, farting, breathing cow
Is more sacred than any statue or sacred cow.

If there is a supreme being of love we worship as the source
Then what made this God? Life on Earth of course!
Religions may teach the after-life is the true and real ideal,
Yet only life in the living body is truly really real.

The dogma of religion is the fifth horseman of this apocalypse
And is just as destructive and evil as corrupt and greedy politics.

Religion preaches animals have no soul
And to worship a disembodied god is the primary goal.
This leads us to abandon our true human fate,
Which is to open our hearts beyond our selves in order to create
A love that embraces all life, not just our own,
And invites every living creature to find a home
In the love within our broken human hearts.
We are then no longer a species apart.

Our love will return us here to where we belong,
To where really we have been living all along,
At one with the flow of life between creatures great and small,
In the interconnected energy field and love of it all.
And because we bring back an even deeper love of life with us,
All life will celebrate our return, welcome and forgive us.

Chorus:
All life is born innocent and naked,
With an instinctive knowledge that only life is sacred.
To give life a purpose beyond itself is irresponsible.
It implies something is more precious than life and that is impossible.

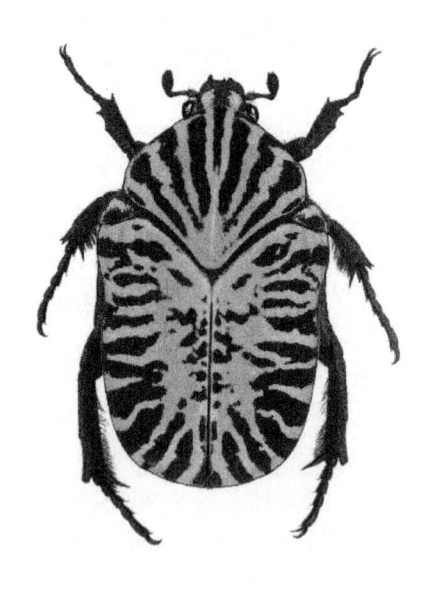

Harlequin Star Beetle

Gymnestis Stellata

BRASSY BIG-EYED BEETLE

Notiophilus Aeneus

From Here to Eternity

Maybe there's even more to this story than has ever been told
And a more numinous complexity to mysteriously unfold.
In which our mammalian warm hearts play a major role
In the creation, evolution and fulfilment of the whole.

First existence came into being with a big bang, or maybe a squeak,
We don't know, though some say God did it all in a week.
Existence became swirling energy and then formed matter,
Protons, neutrons, elements, dark and anti-matter.
This then formed stars, rocks, water, air, all things material,
Until on one small planet, some molecules became bacterial.
No one knows how matter came to life on planet Earth
But it did so, in a fantastical drama of birth, death and rebirth.

The rise of each wave has its individual motion
Before it falls back once more into a oneness with the ocean.
But the ocean is not the same as it was before
That particular wave formed and then washed onto the shore.

Like the wave, all life dies and dissolves back
Into existence for eternity,
Giving itself back into the energy-fields
That shape life's biodiversity.
And the energy of this great body of life can never truly die,
It can only be transformed - there is no ultimate goodbye.

Death is the transition from 'me' to 'us', 'mine' to 'ours',
Where our mortal vulnerability reveals its immortal creative powers,
That each life has meaning beyond its unique experience and soul
In its contribution to the creation and expansion of the whole.
The creative force at work in life's mysterious cycle
Means being alive is about far more than mere survival.

Chorus:
Eternity is not something that's a far off rumour,
We're living in it now; it's not in the future.
Which means how we live here on Earth is profoundly important.
Eternity is being created by us within this very moment.

Kibokoganea Sexmaculata

Kibakoganea Sexmaculata

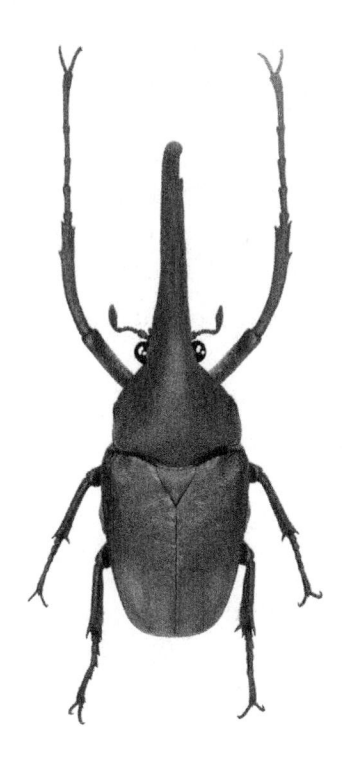

Metallic Green Flower Beetle

Theodosia Viridiaurata

Love's Body

'Eat or be eaten' is the Law of the Jungle.
It's the dialectic of life and the ultimate struggle.
It's how we become each other in a holy communion,
And so death is not separate from life, it's the return to this union.

When we die we give what we are and all we have created
Back to life – the only thing that's sacred.
Our love of life is revealed in our last breath
Because love is the gift of oneself - and that is death.

Our lives are our gift to life, our legacy, our immortality,
And one of the great gifts given to life by mortal humanity
Is that our alienation, brilliant technologies and dark arts
Have created a love of life itself in our broken open hearts.

Our love for all life is a wonderful creation,
It's our fulfilment, our meaning, and our collective liberation.
We may not be able to avert Armageddon and the unfolding tragedy
But we can live through the calamity with love and integrity,
Give ourselves to living fully on this Earth we all inhabit,
And offer to life our love for this unique and beautiful planet.

The mass deaths of the Anthropocene extinction
Will release this love into the energy fields of existence.
Who knows, in the dimensions of energy beyond time and space,
Maybe this love called existence to life in the first place.
What else did? Wandjina, Unkulunkulu, the Spider Grandmother,
Quetzalcoatl, Pangu, Brahma, or some such god or other?

It's a great and challenging paradox
That humanity has struggled with ever since we left paradise:
Death makes life so precious, our love makes us willing to die
To save the lives of those we love so they remain alive.
So however powerful is death, love has the greater power.
It can create the eternity in which all life is ours.

The hero in an Apache legend says, 'This earth is my body,
The sky is my body, the seasons are my body, it is all my body.'
And this body is of love. It is love's body. And it is every body.

Chorus:
Maybe it wasn't divine intervention that shaped this mystery from above
Maybe it was us, all life on Earth - and the power of our love.

Bearded Weevil

Rhinostomus Barbirostris

Roughened Darkling Beetle

Upis Ceramboides

Beyond Tragedy

When we die, if not before, we discover the ultimate reality
That we are and always have been, as is all humanity,
At one with the grass, the flowers, the birds and the trees,
The beetles, the worms, the caterpillars and the bees,
The clouds, the rocks, the rivers and the seas,
The mountain gorillas, the snow leopards, their ticks and their fleas,
The whale in the ocean, the eel in her lake, and the fish in the sea,
Together with the robin who sings her songs in the sycamore tree.

And whether we know it or not, death imparts
That we love this wonderful and terrible life with all our hearts.
And what triumphs over death and all adversity
Is love, the creative force of evolution and eternity.

Our love of life will take us back into the paradise we lost,
When we divided life in order to rule over it at terrible cost.
We can then move beyond the division of life into good and evil
And discover the living knowledge of something more primaeval,
A mystery of the most profound and numinous depth -
That all life is good, even death.

This will return us to the oneness the other animals never left.
And we'll arrive back home, no longer bereft,
Bringing back with us the gifts we created in our long journey away.
And all life will celebrate our return - and this time, we'll stay.

And so even the Anthropocene extinction has meaning in the end
In the vastness of an existence we can never fully comprehend.
Because in the cycle of life ultimately there is no last breath,
Life continually renews itself through the mystery of death.

So let's open our hearts to the mysterious reality
That we are all one body, including humanity.
We belong to one family, with Gaia, our mother,
And other creatures are our kin, we are members of each other.

Which means even in a mass extinction not all we love will die,
Life itself will continue to evolve new forms and thrive.
And in life's renewal through death and then rebirth,
The songs of life will still be sung across the Earth.
And the love we make now will live on in whatever life reforms,
When nature repopulates our planet Earth, its wonders to perform.

American Crudely Carved Wrinkle Beetle

Omoglymmius Americanus

Transvestite Rove Beetle

Leistotrophus Versicolor

The Song

And now let's go again to swim in the songs of lakes,
To sing with the rivers, the stones, the fish, and the snakes,
To lie in singing grass and sing with beetles and bugs,
To sing the songs of mushrooms, insects, hedgehogs and slugs,
To leave the city and take the road into the woods,
To sing with trees the songs of fires and floods,
To sing with octopuses, skylarks, lynx and baboons,
With platypuses, aardvarks, minks and raccoons,
To smell herbs, blow dandelions and lie among ferns and moss,
To sing with them songs of glory, devastation, discovery and loss.
To kneel in fields, smell the soil and sing songs with the ground,
To sing all the songs we lost and then found again in the sound.

Let's sing together the songs of life, of laughter and terrible cruelty,
Of savage magnificence, fierce love and dark unbearable beauty.
For how do we live our wild and precious lives on Earth
If we do not sing of the tragedy of death as well as the joys of birth?

Let's sing and be sung by these songs of wonder and dread.
But let's sing them while we're alive because we can't when we're dead.
Sing until our hearts break and we are left bereft.
Sing until we can sing no more and have no song left.
Sing until we're so lost in the song
We've sung ourselves back to where we belong.
Sing until we no longer sing the song,
The song sings us, as it has done all along.

Then let's leap up and dance in the wind and the rain,
And sing the songs of this beautiful Earth - and then sing them again.

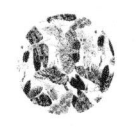

Beetles

Scientists estimate there are over 12 million species of beetle. Over 400,000 beetle species have been documented and described, with more being discovered continually. This makes beetles the largest group of living organisms known to science. Even with plants included in the count, one in every five known organisms is a beetle. One latest calculation is that there are a phenomenal 33 million species of beetle.

Beetles live wherever vegetation is found whether leaves, flowers, trees, bark, underground roots, or dead and decaying plant and fungi tissue of all kinds. They can be found in deserts, tundra, mountains, evergreen forests, deciduous forests, rainforests, coastal habitats, wetlands and grasslands.

Beetles are a group of insects distinguished by the hardened wing-cases on their front wings called elytra. They vary in size from a Feather Wing beetle that is just 0.300 mm long to the Hercules Beetle that reaches 19 cm. They have six jointed legs and three main parts to their body. They also have a pair of antennae. They navigate the world and communicate with each other by using pheromones, sounds and vibrations as well as their eyes.

The oldest known beetle is from around 295 million years ago. Beetles were already in existence before the breakup of the supercontinent Pangaea and they survived the K/T mass extinction that doomed the dinosaurs.

They can survive in a wide variety of environments. The Alaskan beetle (Cucujus clavipes puniceus) is able to withstand −58°C and its larvae can survive the astonishing −100°C. At such low temperatures, the formation of ice crystals in internal fluids is the biggest threat but beetles have found a solution by creating antifreeze proteins that prevent ice forming.

At the other end of the scale, desert dwelling beetles are adapted to tolerate high temperatures. The Tenebrionid beetle, Onymacris rugatipennis, can withstand 50°C. Many desert beetles have developed behavioural adaptations to such heat. Some stand erect on their tarsi (the small segments that make up their feet) to hold their bodies away from the hot ground, others turn to face the sun so that only the front parts of their heads are directly exposed. Others, such as the Fogstand beetle, Stenocara gracilipes, that live in the dry Namib Desert, stand up in the early morning breeze and collect droplets from dawn mist in ridges on their abdomen.

In a very different climate, beetles who live near areas that may flood are able to survive submersion in water without breathing, some for several months.

In their lifetime each beetle undergoes complete metamorphosis. The typical form of metamorphosis in beetles passes through four main stages: the egg, the larva, or grub, the pupa, or chrysalis, and the imago, or adult. And even within the larval stage there can be many changes.

The Blister beetle larva, for example, has at first long legs to search for the eggs of grasshoppers. After feeding for a week, it moults and loses its legs. In another week it changes again into another form of larva, and then a few weeks later again into a pseudo-pupal form to survive the winter. In spring it changes again to pupate until it eventually arrives as the fully formed Blister beetle. At least that's what we call them. With such hypermetamorphosis, as it's called, I doubt beetles suffer much from ego identity crises or care in the slightest what we decide to call them.

Beetles have intricate mating behaviour. They use pheromones to first locate a potential mate. They then engage in complex dialogues with each other, each species using a unique combination of flight patterns, movements and behaviour. Before mating, both male and female beetles often vibrate the objects they are on and if there is no mutual vibration they move away from each other. In many species, if they feel the right vibes, the male climbs onto the back of the female and strokes his antennae on her head, palps, and antennae. Each species has its own particular mating rituals and even within a species there is variation.

In Russia, the Tansy beetle male taps the female's eyes, throat and antennae with its antennae. The tansy beetle in the UK skips this bit. Copulation itself can last a few minutes to several hours. We've more in common with beetles than we think. Though there are other behaviours of beetles that we might wish to emulate but can't.

Many beetles exhibit what is called 'biological immortality'. If starved the beetle larvae can revert to an earlier form. Later they can grow back to maturity with no harmful effects. This cycle can happen over and over for many years. This bio-immortality is thought to be why the scarab beetle was revered in ancient Egypt.

The beetle's capacity to survive in a wide variety of environments is perhaps why they played a significant part in folk medicine all over the world from ancient Chinese medicine, Ayurveda and mediaeval healing in Europe.

In ancient Rome, Pliny suggested you hang dead beetles around the necks of a baby to prevent convulsions. You decapitated the beetle and the longer the head moves when separated from its body, the more potent the remedy.

Bald's Leechbook (compiled in the ninth century) describes many beetle remedies such as the wearing of the head of a beetle as an amulet and hung round the necks of children, to protect from evil forces, epileptic seizures, bedwetting and cramp. Crushed beetles were used for bruises, gout, growths, earache and dealing with cases of poisoning. It was also thought that wearing beetles in your hair protects against more general pain, headache, oedema, rheumatism, nervous disorders and to ease childbirth. Though you'd have thought a bunch of beetles crawling on your scalp might give you a headache rather than curing one.

Leechbook III also describes some beetle magic. One procedure involves a dung beetle. "You must first grab the dung beetle with two hands along with its dung-ball. Wave greatly with your hands and say three times: Remedium facio ad ventris dolorem (I make a cure for the pain in the stomach). Throw then the beetle over your shoulder onto the path. See to it that you do not look back. In case of a person's stomach or abdomen pain, grab with your hands the stomach. It will soon be whole for them." This procedure allegedly gave the practitioner the ability to cure stomach aches for a whole year, after which presumably you had to go through the whole procedure all over again.

Beetles had healing properties but were also considered dangerous. The sudden appearance of beetles was believed to herald a terrible storm. A beetle near your house was inviting lightening to strike. If one entered your home while you and your family were seated, bad luck would follow. And if you killed a beetle inside your home, someone would die within a year.

Some were called Devil's Imps and were believed to have been dispatched from hell to cause trouble by eating crops, carrying fire up to attics to burn down houses and driving people mad by climbing through their ears into their brains. Then again, if you found a beetle stuck on its back and righted it, you purged yourself of sin and all your time in purgatory was wiped. Until you next sinned, which wouldn't be long.

Beetles were often associated with death. Particularly the Death Watch beetle. These bore holes into wood and bang their heads against the inside of the holes, particularly in the rafters of houses. They make this noise to find a mate. But when people held vigils at the bedside of the dead or dying, the ticking became synonymous with death, as most of the time folk were usually out and about working in the fields so didn't hear them. Many thought the sound was the grim reaper tapping his fingers while he waited impatiently for another soul to escort to either hell or purgatory, unless you were a saint and scheduled straight for the harp playing on clouds.

Whether harbingers of death, healing remedies for convulsions or suppliers of magical powers, we owe our lives to beetles. Before flying insects could fertilise plants, beetles did the job. One of the first flowering plants were magnolia trees. Beetles fertilised these and so played a major role in the evolution of the wonderful variety of plants, trees, bushes, flowers, grasses and herbs that we have today, at least for a while longer. Without beetles we would not be here at all. So thank you, beetles. Sorry for ripping your heads off to wear in our hair, selling you live in vending machines as toys, spraying you with insecticide, destroying your forest homes and sticking you in containers to see how long you could live without air or food.

Maybe beetles can take consolation in that their remarkable powers of adaptation and bio-immortality mean some of them may still be here long after we have gone.

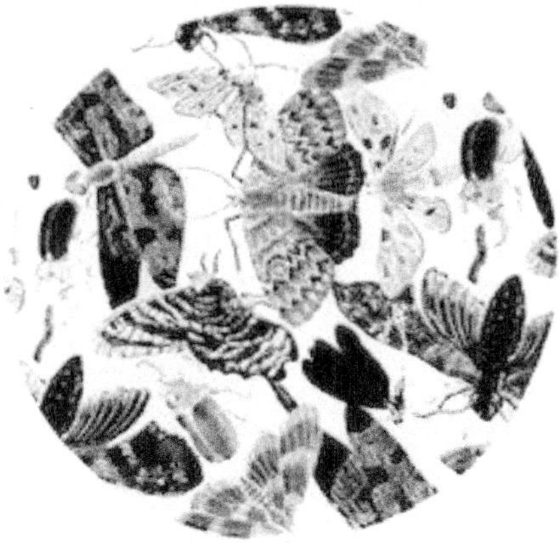

Printed in Great Britain
by Amazon